THREE INSPIRED BOOKS THAT CAN HELP YOU LIVE YOUR MAGNIFICENCE

THE PRINCESS | THE JOURNEY | THE WAY HOME

GINNY DREWES
MAGNIFICENCE COACH

THE PRINCESS | THE JOURNEY | THE WAY HOME

By GINNY DREWES

Copyright © 2007 by Ginny Drewes
Cover Design by Lizann Michaud www.michaud-design.com
Layout Design by BMS

Published by: **BookMarketingSolutions** LLC

10300 E. Leelanau Court
Traverse City, Michigan 49684
  orders@BookMarketingSolutions.com
  www.BookMarketingSolutions.com
  Phone 231-929-1999

Printed in the United States of America

Drewes, Ginny.
   The princess; the journey; the way home : three inspired books that
   can help you live your magnificence / Ginny Drewes, Magnificence
   Coach. -- Traverse City, Mich. : BookMarketingSolutions, 2007.
       p. ; cm.
       ISBN-13: 978-0-9790834-9-5
       ISBN-10: 0-9790834-9-4
       1. Women--Psychology. 2. Self-esteem in women. 3. Selfperception
   in women. 4. Self-actualization (Psychology)
       5. Achievement motivation in women. I. Title. II. Title: Journey.
   III. Title: Way home.
HQ1206 .D74 2007

158.1/082--dc22   0710

This book is available at ReadingUp.com

DEDICATION

This book is dedicated to Randolph Wilkinson, a man who helped me remember I was "a flower in God's garden" when I could only imagine myself as a "weed." His message was simple, clear, and absolute: We are all God's children, we are all magnificent, and there is no argument about that for it is not ours to decide. He accepted me totally while challenging me to live my best life. I am not alone in appreciating what he was here to give, and in my challenging moments his message still rings in my ears. I am forever grateful for his words and his unconditional love for all! I don't miss you, Randolph, because I know you are just somewhere waiting for all of us. Thank you for being in my mind and heart as I continue my journey.

Acknowledgements

I am grateful to Dr. Dave Rankin and the MLA program at Winthrop University for giving me the platform to explore this concept, and to Dr. Shelley Hamill and Dr. Lois Veronen for believing in me, supporting and guiding my work.

Thank you to Shadow Work, Inc., Cliff Barry, Vicki Woodard, Alyce Barry, John Miller, Jeff Foster and Delynn Copley for their guidance, connection, ongoing training and coaching, and to Janine Romaner, thank you for showing up in my life as a friend and mentor. I appreciate Helene Van Manen of Retreat Coaches, for her leadership and support of my project and her "grandmother" friendship.

Thank you Judy Tillotson for advice along the way, for reading and comments, and general "believing in me" support. Nancy Doyle and Patricia Vane have been friends, readers and listeners and carried excitement about this project that helped me stay focused.

I am thankful, too, for my friends Rachel Rogers, Karen Gilson and Peggy Payne, who have supported my work at Safe Passage and helped me put theory into practice. And to Bill Browning for the technical advice that made these ideas accessible.

For suggesting ideas that have brought this book forward to be more than I ever thought it could be, I so appreciate Tom White's help.

To my children, Julie, Bill, and Nancy, thank you for helping me believe in magnificence. And to Michelle, Todd, and Ben, thank you for coming into my life and bringing little Sabra, Alexis and Lila—you are all capable of living beautiful dreams. Always remember the light I see in you because you are here.

My sister Nancy and I have talked things over for years, and in that rich conversation, some of the seeds of this book sprouted. I hold that connection very dear. I am also grateful to my husband, Charlie, who has believed in me and helped me climb out of the pain of the past, into a world where anything is possible.

Introduction to the Trilogy

The Princess, The Journey, and *The Way Home* is a trilogy designed to softly carry you through tragedy, struggle, or relationship loss and remind you of who you are. Its simple message can be heard in the middle of pain and can hold you gently. Its deeper message will appeal to an inner part of you longing to hear and remember your value long after you have lost its truth. In all, it will help you return home to your true Self!

This book will fit nicely on a nightstand, to be read before drifting off into dreams. Or it can be gifted to someone you know who is in need of remembering that life can be different, filled instead with joy, gratitude, and the awareness of their own magnificence.

When I wrote this book, a friend who had known me well, suggested this was the story of my life. I did not want to hear that. Perhaps denying my struggle could make it less real. Yet, it was my story. I carried wounds from my childhood in the form of barriers to loving and believing in myself. There were times I did not want to keep going, my pain was so real, it blocked out the possibility of healing. And now, when I work with clients, and the women of Safe Passage, I hold the truth of healing potential for them. This is a book that validates pain, a necessary step to healing, and gently holds the truth that you cannot only survive, you can soar. This is the book I was looking for when I felt so lost. May it remind you of your magnificence and may you know who you are. Your original magnificence can be forgotten—it cannot be destroyed.

ABOUT *THE PRINCESS*

This project was an opportunity for me to present ideas I have had and to create something easily read by people who are in the midst of struggle. The first book, *THE PRINCESS*, was written as I sat down with my journal. The words just kept flowing through me and I had to stop and read the story I had written. *THE PRINCESS* found me and has been a foundation for much of the work I do with women.

THE
PRINCESS

Once upon a time, a Princess was born into a Kingdom. She was truly blessed, for this was the most beautiful Kingdom of all.

The nursery where she slept had the finest of everything. Her bassinet had a canopy of silk. Only the most luxurious fabrics touched her skin. The carpet in her room was the thickest that could be found so she would never be disturbed. Constant guardians surrounded her to attend to her every need and assure the King and Queen of her safety.

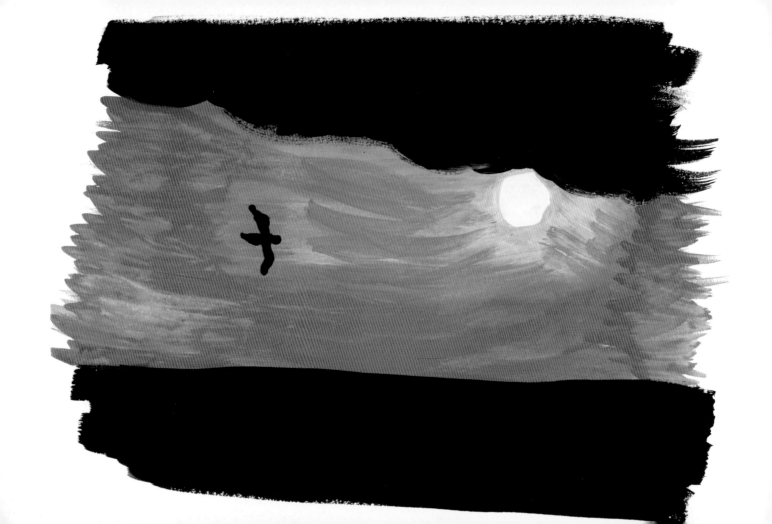

One evening as the Princess lay sleeping, she was spirited away. As tiny as she was, she didn't realize she had been taken from the Kingdom. While there were people who cared for her, and many of her needs were met, something very warm and safe was missing.

The Kingdom was in an uproar. Where was the Princess? Where had she gone? Years went by and the search continued until one day, the King received word that the Princess had been found. Yet he was a wise King and he knew the Truth—the Princess could only return home if she chose to come home. But time spent in the new place had left her unaware of her real home, confused about her vague sense of loss, and wondering who she was.

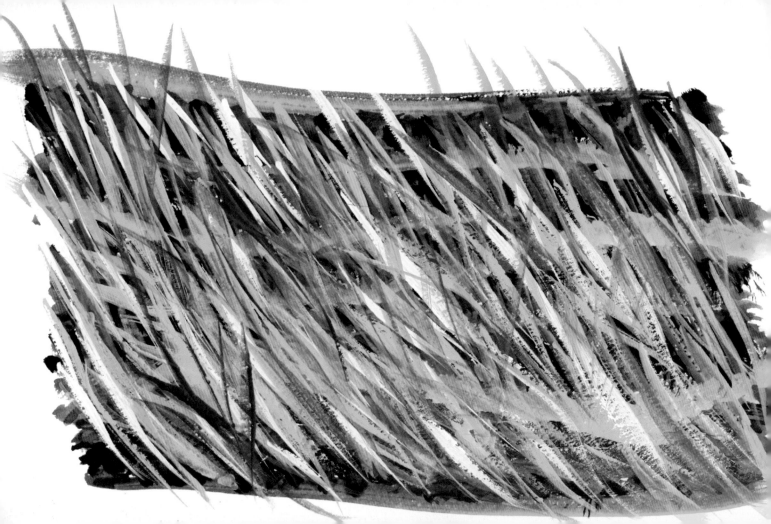

*S*o the King called together the greatest thespians of his Kingdom for he had devised a plan. He would send these messengers to the Princess to help her remember her real home. Once the Princess remembered who she was, the King knew she would come running home—she would realize she was a Princess and that she belonged in the Kingdom.

The meeting commenced and the King outlined his plan for the thespians. He explained that the messages had to be subtle, as time spent in the new place had frightened the Princess and she had begun to build a special protection around her tender heart.

As the king assigned everyone a part, some of the thespians complained. They all wanted to play happy roles, and the King explained: when people forget their magnificence they must be reminded gently. They often argue for their limitations and dismiss joy. We can remain loving and meet her where she is. As she becomes less afraid, you can play happier roles and continue to help her remember.

And the thespians loved the King and the Princess so much they agreed to do what they were asked.

*F*or many years the messengers visited the Princess and gradually she began to listen to the urgings of her heart. She started to see through the roles the messengers were playing and became less afraid of them. In quiet times and in the night, she listened to the stirrings in her Be-ing. And when she heard particular melodies or saw certain cloud formations, she opened up a little more. Once, a hummingbird came right up to her face and hovered for a few seconds, sending tremendous joy through the Princess. She had begun her journey home.

As the days went by, the Princess became more and more aware that an amazing peace had come over her. The times of fear were fewer and far between, and when they came upon her, she knew how to get quiet and listen. She began to once again know she was a Princess and that her true parents were the King and Queen. All that was left was to go home.

The celebration was grand when the Princess returned to the Kingdom. What gifts the King and Queen had for her! What parties! What a blessed event it was! Her days were spent in excited anticipation of the surprises and experiences ahead. The Princess was safe—she was finally home.

About *The Journey*

As we begin to take a look at ourselves and the choices we make that create our lives, we may find that events in our childhood helped form the images we have about ourselves today. Our willingness to reach for higher rewards, to believe in our dreams, and to imagine our lives without limits is often dependent on what our caregivers believed about themselves.

But what if we were free of that beginning and could jump over any barriers?

The Princess had forgotten who she was. How many of us have found ourselves in that same position of forgetting our original magnificence? We experience life from a perspective of lack and limitation, or struggle, and do not realize there is another approach. It may take us years to find our way.

The Journey, part two of the trilogy, answered a question for me. I had wondered what had happened in the life of the Princess between forgetting who she was and remembering. *The Journey* filled in this gap by telling the story of a woman, any woman really, from the time she is a small child to when she seeks help and eventually triumphs. I wanted to have spaces between the stories of her life to suggest years passing and decided to present lessons to alternate with the stories. The lessons and the stories are different fonts.

THE
JOURNEY

The Lesson

We are born magnificent and then it is gone. That knowing, that awareness of greatness slips away. Were we grabbed up and spirited away from it or did it leave us? Either way, we will spend years with an underlying ache, a loss so profound it hurts.

We lose our sense of magnificence in small ways. We have a deep, longing need to connect, to be part of the world. But instead of being accepted for who we are, we are made to fit into what is already there.

If our caregivers remembered who they were, magnificent beings, our birth would probably have been something they consciously chose. They might have watched us and listened to our every sound. Every choice we made might have been heralded and validated as ours, part of our unique way of being. They might have shared our excitement about life.

The Story

She felt cold. There was sadness all around. The people in her life carried burdens. It wasn't as though there were actual bags on their backs, but she could see the burdens just the same.

The other day on her way home from school, she saw a beautiful leaf. She had been walking by a puddle, looking at the way the sky and the trees reflected in it, like an upside-down mirror. It was easy to get lost in the wonder of it all. Then a leaf just fell from the sky into the middle of the puddle. She picked it up, dried it off with her skirt, and carried it safely home. There were colors in that leaf she had never seen before, and the way it was shaped, like a hand just reaching out to help. It made her feel so good, even a little mysterious. She wanted to share it, this wondrous gift that had fallen to her. But the house was dark when she got home, and she remembered Mom was sick again. It somehow felt wrong to be happier than Mom. So she put the leaf between the pages of her favorite book for safekeeping.

The Lesson

Our lives are filled with judgments. We learn very early how to judge and we cringe daily on the chance we may BE judged. Our refuge is in our sameness — if we are exactly like everyone else we may escape. And the unique, beautiful girl who used to be me is silenced, buried and ignored. The tragedy is, our public self, the self we want others to see, seems to have no choice but to arrange and carry out the burial, close the door on our magnificence, then turn away as our uniqueness is stilled. We try desperately to be what we think our parents, teachers, and others want us to be. The unique magnificence — that precious girl who once was — is lost, taking with it our sense of value and worth.

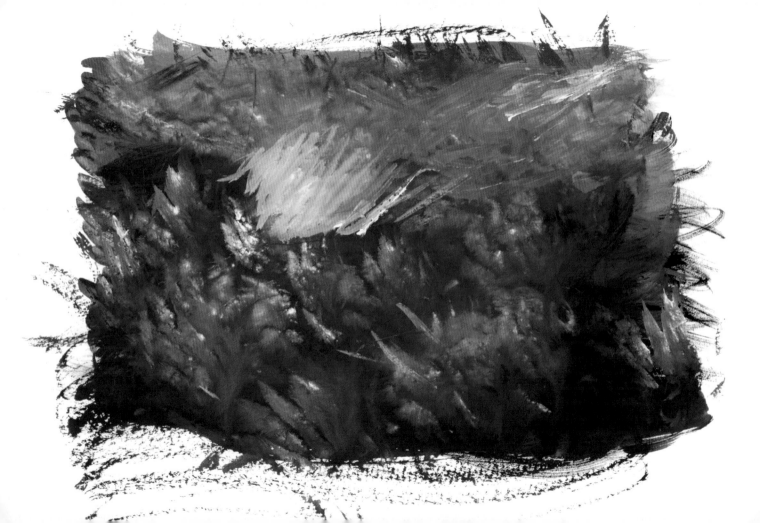

The Story

The boxes were almost loaded. The new apartment would be okay, at least that was what she kept telling herself. It was a lot smaller than this one, but she could never afford to stay here with her roommate moving out. If she had received that promotion, and there had been a chance, she would have that new job and things would be different. She had really wanted it. The day she heard about it, she got excited. She had held up the announcement and smiled, and for a moment she knew she could have it. But by the time she got home, those voices in her head had convinced her she didn't have a chance. She folded the announcement and put it in the letter box on her desk.

The Lesson

We might see that part of us in our dreams, the part that knows she is royal, sacred, and grand. We seldom see her in waking times. We don't really want to see her and be reminded of how far we've moved away from our center. We've buried the longing for her with busy-ness, substances, shopping, or losing ourselves in another person a new career, another degree, a new dress . . .

The Story

At times she almost felt there was an argument going on in her head—different voices talking to her at the same time. She had a dream the other night. It was one of those dreams she remembered and felt all day. Two people were arguing. One looked a little like Dad, the other Mom. Dad was telling Mom she couldn't make it without him, no one would pay any attention to her, and she wasn't smart enough to get a job that would pay her any money. When Mom started to cry, he laughed at her. He was still laughing when Mom crumpled on the floor into the puddle of tears and disappeared.

She had woken up with a start, breathing hard. Her husband was gone, up and off to work. It was getting light outside. She helped the children get off to school. A magazine fell open at her feet to a picture of a little girl standing in a puddle. She tore the picture out, clutched it to her, and sobbed sobs that came from somewhere deep inside her. It was getting late. She folded the picture and put it in her closet under her sweaters.

The Lesson

Searching outside is not the way to reach her, that magnificent self, that self that dances and is filled with passionate expression of who she really is. She can only be reached by going inside, and it often takes work to push through the dark shadow patterns of who she's become. It is a journey of courage, not for the faint-hearted. It is often a lonely journey, yet it is a journey best taken with someone who has gone before us and champions our way. Many watch us prepare for the challenges—Shadow Work, therapy, workshops, high ropes— and are filled with fear and awe and a question: "Can I do this for myself?"

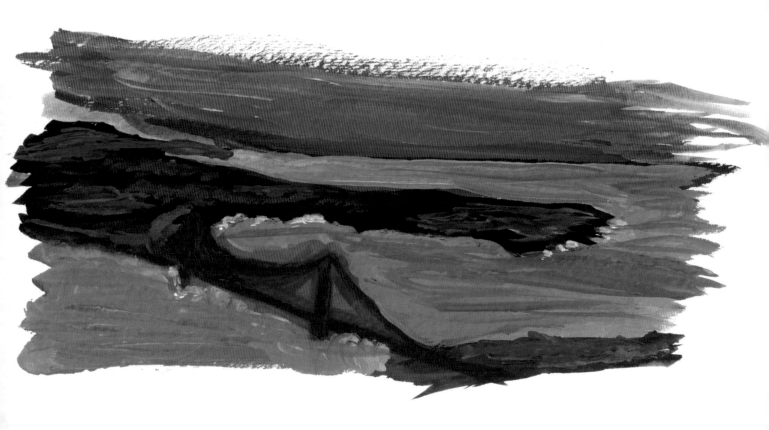

The Story

The sun was setting as the airplane ascended. She could see the Golden Gate Bridge below. It always made her smile, reminding her of safe harbor. She had been visiting her sister, deciding what to do. Her marriage was over, she was free—that was one way to look at it. There were so many sharp pains connected to seeing her situation for what it really was. She felt as if her skin were reversed and the raw nerve endings were touching her clothing and the air. She had thrown her wedding ring into the bay one day and walked away lighter.

In a park near her sister's house, she would sit on a bench near a eucalyptus tree and watch the bay below. She was lost in the fragrance and the beauty of the sailboats on the water one day when a hummingbird stopped and hovered right in front of her face. She could not move; it felt joyful and astounding all at once.

The Lesson

We peel off one layer of the onion at a time. There are deep parts we cannot see until we break through to them. We must become disenchanted with wanting more toys, more degrees, more relationships, and we must break through the fog that addictive substances create in our lives.

She's standing there, waiting. And when we first see her, she may be petulant, angry that we have taken so long to reach her. How could we have ignored our own greatness, our magnificence? It is a part of us we cannot destroy or invalidate. We can only forget, and when we are willing to remember, there she stands, in all her glory, ready to be adored. She is waiting for us to watch her and delight in what she wants to be and feel.

The Story

She knew she needed help. Does anyone find their way alone? Why had she resisted? The workshop was in Colorado and she was pulling into the grounds of the Living Sanctuary. A sign beside the road read "Expect a Miracle." It felt like a miracle just to be there. Even renting the car was a frightening event. She had been so afraid she wanted to turn around, but she had come this far and had nowhere else to go.

She parked the car near the sign that said "Registration." As she walked toward the door, another sign read "You Know the Truth — Remember!!!" And suddenly she did remember. She had only forgotten. She had forgotten who she was. She stopped and listened to the birds singing and saw the flowers lining the walkway. She looked at her hand pulling the suitcase. What a miracle!

The Lesson

It takes courage to remember her, that magnificent girl, and faith that she still exists after all the years of being hidden away. Shine the light, let it lead the way. It is your radiance, your magnificence that is calling. It smiles at the judgments of others, it laughs in the face of adversity, and it loves. Oh, how it loves. The chains that bound your heart have been broken and it is free to beat in joy. There are ways to the top of the mountain that won't require struggle and the choice is yours, independent of anyone else.

Dance, dance with her in wild abandon. You are magnificent! You are a Princess. The Princess is free and she knows she is grand. Long live the Princess!

The Story

The house of cards she had built her life upon had come tumbling down. She hadn't even noticed other materials were available. She could see it now though, the richness of possibilities were surrounding her. It was a new day and the sky was the limit. There was peace. There was joy. It was time.

... and the celebration was grand!!!

ABOUT *THE WAY HOME*

THE WAY HOME, book three in the triology, is a collection of poems I wrote during times of struggle and times of light — I have experienced both. As I reread these poems, I often go back to those days of when I seemed to be in pain. They were dark days, yet survivable. In fact, they were necessary for me to learn what I needed to know so that I could fulfill my own purpose.

Now I watch women in the midst of their struggles and I understand they can not only overcome obstacles but triumph if they believe in themselves. There are many beautiful women at the shelter who have helped me see the value of remembering that magnificence, and as I watch the courage they exhibit, I am renewed in my own belief.

THE
WAY HOME

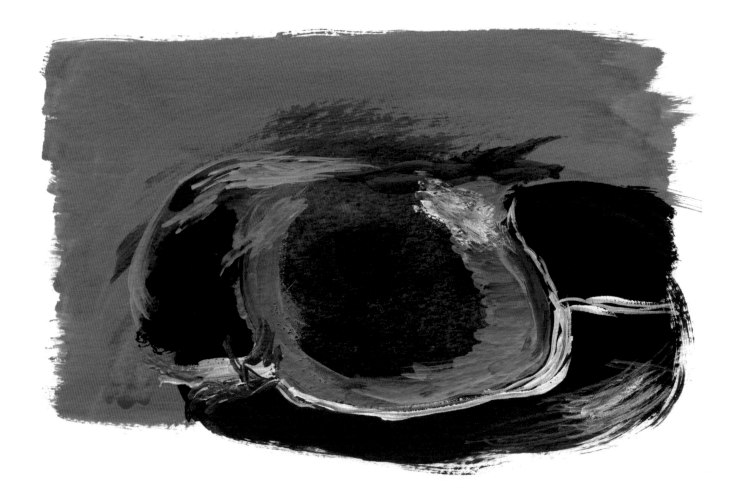

I was in a deep, dark hole and I wanted out.
I could see the light but couldn't get a grip.
How long had I been in that hole without knowing there WAS a way out?
When I see the light and want to reach it, the path appears.
I become aware.
Bring up the truth, spin it, see it for what it is and the part it has played in this experience of being in a deep, dark hole.

There was a moment when everything seemed to stop.
I was afraid and not sure of how to go on or if I wanted to.
Yet I could never have known, could never have grown in this way without that moment.

Self-discovery can be difficult or exciting:
it all depends on our perception.

*I*magine receiving an invitation to a new reality show—"The Princess."

You agree to spend one year of your life living with "someone" on a remote island.
You are picked up and whisked away in a private jet to an elegant, far-removed location.
Your task is to really get to know this "someone."

As the curtain goes up on this person you will get to know so well,
you see it is the self you could have been if you had never forgotten the Truth about you.

She is glorious.
She shines with a light that has never been hidden.
She moves with the grace of self-assurance.
And she is eager to reveal her magnificence.

Struggle or light are choices.
The decision as to which one wins is dependent on my willingness to really see myself.

Look in the mirror, child. What do you see?
Do you see anger, sorrow, regret, greed, arrogance, self-pity, guilt, resentment,
inferiority, lies, false pride, or envy?

Or—
Do you see joy, peace, love, hope, serenity, compassion, benevolence, empathy,
generosity, truth, faith, kindness, or humility?

A wounded animal must lash out and curls into its darker side.
The pain it feels finds reasons for blame and shame.

Healing comes in our willingness to see.
You might use the mirror vision of seeing others and recognizing your own likeness.
The question is, do I "support" the woundedness or do I "support" the healing?

I had a dream.

I needed to climb a mountain. There was something up there I needed to get.

A sign at the bottom of the mountain

—THIS WAY TO THE TOP OF THE MOUNTAIN—

led me to the right.

I began my climb.

It was steep, and at times I was digging my feet into cliff face

and holding on to roots to pull myself up.

I was bruised and bleeding and exhausted when I finally slung myself over the top.

As I lay there, catching my breath, I saw a trolley dropping people off.

Incredulous, I drug myself to the trolley and climbed on for the ride down.

There had been another sign

—THE WAY TO THE TOP OF THE MOUNTAIN, BY TROLLEY, FOR FREE—

But I had chosen the struggle.

I thought I should be happy.
I made excuses and shamed myself for being dissatisfied.
If I had known it was the Princess within me sending messages that she wanted out,
I might have moved more quickly.

I didn't willingly let her out.
I waited until I was broken.
That is often the way.

*I*n the stillness, in the quiet times, I am one.
This is not an easy place to find.
I must want it very much
or be broken.

I ran along the road—I was trying to keep up.
I could go no further, a raging forest fire blocked my way.
So I turned to the right and ran along the road, still trying to keep up.
A hungry tiger stood in my way.
So I turned again and ran along the road until I reached a wall and could go no further.
I turned again and there was a cliff.

I'm not running anymore.
But I might fly.

I had no idea.
I had no idea.
The expression of what I want,
the freedom to express it,
the power I felt when I let it go
was like taking flight and soaring over the Grand Canyon of my life.
I could see the broken places and marvel at the way the magnificence had been molded.
A symphony began to play and I knew it was one of a kind, so unique
it lifted me up to soar even higher.
I had no idea.

Wake up, wake up.
Don't leave her behind.
Take the time, set the stage.
Watch and listen.
She will reveal herself to you if she sees she is welcome.
She will sing for you if you love her song.
And you will see the light within you has been there all along.
Don't waste time in sadness or shame that it took so long.
Just get her out.
Let her dance and dance and dance and dance.

She did her best, there is no shame.
The odds seemed insurmountable to her,
yet she did the best she could and she's still here.
There was little light to see with
yet she did the best she could.
She was a warrior burdened with armor, judged and found wanting,
yet she struggled on and did the best she could.
And there were times she could see the light and she wanted to fly.
And she was strong and she loved, and that was why she did the best she could.
THAT IS ENOUGH.

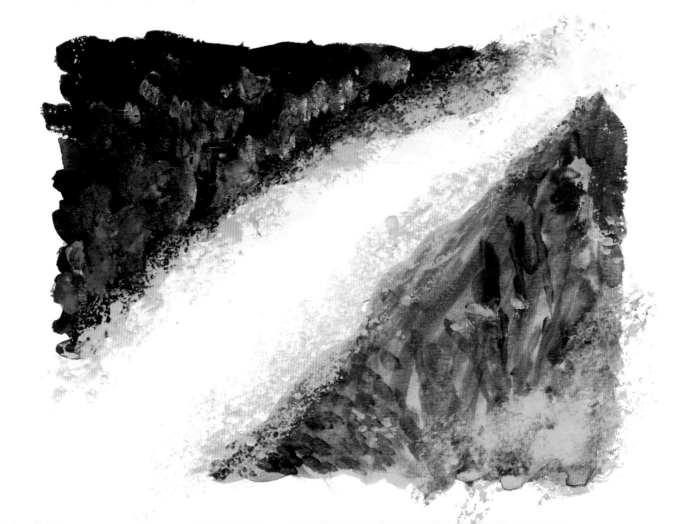

If the river is always still,
I do not know my strength against the current.
I will go nowhere,
and the fiber of my being has no opportunity to thicken.

I did what they said.
I thought it was what they wanted.
No one seemed happy.
No one said, "Okay, great, that's exactly it. You are so perfect for doing what I wanted."
I thought I would be so happy if someone noticed what I had done.
I thought I would be so happy if someone noticed me at all.
I learned to stuff and ignore my feelings.
I learned that happiness is hard in the face of pain and struggle.
I learned I can be no happier than the least happy person in my life.

How do I find my way?
So many days and nights of looking when I don't really want to see.
I want the Truth pushed down where it's been all these years!
No need of it coming up now and getting in the way of my plans.
Ah, my plans.
Those plans I have—they help me breathe.
They are my reason for being.
Who am I if no one sees me, and who would see me without my plans?
So I run and run and run.
I don't have time to stop right now, but someday I will—
you just watch.

The shadow side of myself!
It has held on with the tenacity of an octopus.
If one tentacle released there were at least four more tightly binding me.
I could pretend it was "them" for a while.
They were ignoring me, they were limiting me, I was unable to move very much at all.
I would love to be all I can be but you can surely see how "they" are holding me back.
The hold is so strong, can't you see, I'm so unable to really be who I am.
"You understand, don't you?"

And I move on with the tentacles gripping, squeezing more and more life out of all that I am.

When the Phoenix rises out of the ashes does she stop to analyze the fire?
She has no time. She's been in the flame too long.
Don't hold her back a second longer.
The release is total, it is free.
To look back now would be a delay unbearable,
a loss of time unconscionable.

I would never fear loss if:
I knew there was more where that came from;
I knew I could only lose what I needed to lose to grow;
I knew I was magnificent;
I knew I was powerfully skilled and talented;
I knew healthy people were available and could not resist me.

Expecting someone to think exactly as you do
is expecting them to willingly ignore the sum total of their life experiences
and accept the sum total of your experiences
without the dance.

I was a kitten, a pet really, and in so many ways naïve.

I chose to be naïve, yet it didn't seem like a choice then.

I didn't realize I had options. Choosing meant responsibility.

I did not want the responsibility. I did not know I had the courage to be responsible.

Courage was for people who were facing survival challenges.

Survival was not the issue.

My home was beyond average.

My children were healthy, intelligent, and attractive, and we were all nice people.

We had cars, electronics, and appliances. It was a life many wish for.

I had no right to be dissatisfied.

I know now:

A dissatisfied, unfulfilled spirit makes itself known, in one form or another.

A heart must dance, a spirit must soar, and the inner voice must sing.

We do an amazing job of shutting this down by the time we reach our teens.

We do such thorough work of it that we don't even know it has happened.

The lights are turned off gradually so we can become accustomed to the darkness …
and think it is real.

A woman in American culture learns very early
to pay attention to the preferences of those around her.
I wanted to be a good daughter—I listened hard so I would know how.
I wanted to be a good wife—I tried to give my husband what he wanted.
I wanted to be a good mother—I thought I knew what my children wanted.
One day I was alone. It was earlier than I had expected.
Making a new life requires goals and dreams.
Yet my goals and dreams had been hidden away for so long they were reluctant to surface.
It will catch up with you one day when someone asks the seemingly simple question—
"WHAT WOULD YOU LIKE TO DO?"
And you realize you could answer that question for every other person, yet not for yourself.

It is time to fly, little bird.
Don't wait for the dew to dry on the rose petals in the sun.
Don't wait for the tree to shade the afternoon.
Don't wait for the moon to open its eyes and watch you sleep.
Your wings have grown strong, your vision has cleared.
Your heart beating passionately in your chest has waited so long, so long.
It is time to fly, little bird.
And I will watch you rise tentatively at first, until you catch the wind …
and soar …
and I will smile!

Final Thought

I have come to believe I can change what I do —
I cannot change who I am.
Isn't it great that who I AM is magnificent?
I need only remember!

A portion of the author's proceeds will go to Safe Passage,
a domestic violence shelter for women and children in Rock Hill, South Carolina.

Author's Note

Three years ago I did a project for my graduate study at Withrop University with the women from Safe Passage. What began as a one semester project continued beyond the school year.

A woman who experiences domestic violence will often arrive at the door of Safe Passage with nothing but herself, her children, the clothes on her back and what she could quickly gather. In her eyes, she has lost esteem for the very act of having to ask for this help. She must now live with other women and children who also have emotional pain many of us could never imagine. Her act of coming to Safe Passage is an extreme act of courage yet when I suggest this to the women, they tell me it doesn't feel like courage—it feels like failure.

For the protection of the residents, the location of Safe Passage is not common knowledge. Is it possible that we have hidden away these women and children because it is not easy for us to recognize our own responsibility as our sister's keeper? Our community will be the better for "adopting" the residents in such a way as to support their progress from "courage to leave domestic violence" to "ability to be successful."

Ginny Drewes is a certified Shadow Work® coach and facilitator and a certified retreat coach. She has specialized in helping women and men grow their deep connection to their magnificence. Ginny offers coaching and retreats for individuals and groups. She has led creative programs of change for adults in relationship recovery, women in crisis pregnancy, and domestic violence shelters.

Ginny has a master's degree in liberal arts and has concentrated her studies in wellness and health education. She has been a Course in Miracles student for 12 years and much of her work expresses her spiritual connection. Ginny's work reflects her belief that much of our wounding has happened because we were shamed, and healing requires a connection with someone in our corner who is willing to support us in a shame-free way.

Ginny and her husband, Charles, live in South Carolina within easy reach of her three children and three grandchildren.

Additional copies of this book
and other titles by BMS are
available at ReadingUp.com
or your local bookstore.

If you have enjoyed this book, or it has impacted your life, we would like to hear from you!
If you are interested in retreats that support this message, contact us at:

magjan1@aol.com
or phone us at 980-722-0252.

<u>Ginny offers retreats on the following subjects</u>:
Are You Living the Life You Want?
Relationship NO to Relationship YES!
Find Your Power — Live Your Authentic Life!
Parent–Preschool Classes
Princess Retreat — Remember Who You Really Are!

You can co-create the perfect retreat for yourself or your group, or check the schedule at
www.liveyourmagnificence.com for scheduled opportunities.